MW01625071

The 5 Best Decisions THE BEATLES Ever Made...

A Handbook for "Top of the Charts" Success

by
Bill Stainton

Illustrations by
Court Jones

Little Creek Press

Seattle, WA

Raves for Bill's Keynote Presentation:

The 5 Best Decisions The Beatles Ever Made...and Why You Should Make Them Too!

"Bill Stainton was terrific—funny, interesting, and entertaining. He provided fun facts regarding the Beatles and application of their success for us to use now."

Barbara Hensley
Heller Ehrman White & McAuliffe

"Baby, you can drive my car...your presentation rocked. I wish you could have talked longer. Fascinating."

Nancy Kincl
Vulcan Capital

"Very motivational and encouraging. I found the information provided was relevant both personally and professionally. The information was delivered in a manner that kept it fun and interesting! Great presentation. The best this year!"

Rich Boswell
Raynier Institute & Foundation

"Not only does Bill know everything about the Beatles (we couldn't stump him...and we tried!), but he also knows how to translate their success to the world of business. It's a surprisingly good mix. The thought provoking business messages make his presentation valuable; the Beatles stories make it fun!"

Lauriann Reynolds
PEMCO Mutual Insurance

"An informative program that appeals to all ages and to any organization. Practical, yet entertaining. By far our best program of the year!"

Ellen Callahan
Seattle Housing Authority

"Loved his presentation—it was so much more than I expected. I appreciated the fact that Bill included current information as well."

Margie Byrne
Federal Reserve Bank

"I really enjoyed Bill's presentation concerning the Beatles. It was informative and entertaining, with some hard-hitting realities on management and leadership qualities that makes it relevant to today's business climate. Since the presentation, I keep a copy of the '5 Decisions' on my desk."

Ronald S. Grasgreen
WestCoast Hotels

"It's interesting, intriguing, compelling, and engaging. You learn what the best in the business did...and how it also makes sense for your business. Plus, you'll learn all over again why you so enjoy hearing Twist and Shout!"

Brian Walter
The Effectiveness Institute

"Bill's extraordinary knowledge about the Beatles and his passion for this subject were evident, and he was able to convey his message in an entertaining and educational manner, with just the right amount of humor and audience participation."

Mary Rosen
International Association of Administrative Professionals

THE 5 BEST DECISIONS THE BEATLES EVER MADE

ISBN: 978-0-9797503-0-4

Printed in the United States of America

Published by:

Little Creek Press

Seattle, WA

Ordering Information

To order more copies of this book please contact:

1-888-5BEATLE

Also by Bill Stainton

Humor Us!
America's Funniest Humorists on the Power of Laughter

Bombproofing:
How to Use Humor on the Platform Without Falling on Your Face

Acknowledgments

The great poet, John Donne, once wrote, "No man is an island." But then Simon & Garfunkle sang, "I am a rock, I am an island." So who knows? The point is, this book is not mine alone, and I owe a few debts of gratitude to some folks who, knowingly or unknowingly, helped me along the way:

My family, whose inquisitive minds and whose own books (much, *much* thicker than this) have been a constant inspiration throughout my life.

My friends at NSA, too numerous to name, who encouraged and/or shamed me into finally putting words to paper.

Court Jones, whose wonderful illustrations grace the pages and cover of this book. Check out more of his inventive artwork at www.courtjones.com.

The late Bob Wooler, former DJ at the Cavern Club who introduced the Beatles 292 times, and who, over more pints of beer than I can count, shared many private Beatles stories...several of which he made me promise never to tell.

All the musicians I've played with over the years. From each of you I've learned something about music and life. And we did some good Beatles covers too!

And, of course, the Fab Four: the Beatles. For the music, the memories, and the message.

For all my audiences

who have been encouraging me to put this message into book form for many years.

Contents

Introduction

February 9th, 1964. That was the day that I became a Beatles fan. I was six and a half years old, sound asleep in my bed, when my mom—in what was an unusually hip move for her—woke me up. Apparently, there was something on TV that she thought I might like to see. Something from England. Something called...the Beatles?

On that Sunday evening, I joined 73 million other Americans who were watching *The Ed Sullivan Show*. And, like many of them, I became a Beatles fan that day.

I don't think it was the music—not yet, at least. It probably wasn't the hair—although I clearly remember laughing myself silly because it seemed so *long* (times change, don't they?). To be honest, I'm not sure what it was that turned me into a Beatles fan that day. They just had...something.

I've subsequently spent many years analyzing the many "somethings" that made the Beatles what they were. I've never grown tired of reading about them (and it seems there's a new Beatles book every week!); I've never grown tired of talking for hours on end with other "Beatle people;" and, of course, I've never grown tired of listening to the music. I've never stopped being a fan.

BUT WHY A BUSINESS BOOK ABOUT THE BEATLES?

I'm not naïve (at least, that's what I naively tell myself). I realize that not *everybody* is a Beatles fan. My friend Chris, in fact, *hates* the Beatles! Does this make him wrong? Well, quite frankly...yes. But that may just be my bias showing. The fact remains, there are some people who just don't care for the Beatles. They don't like the Beatles' music, their politics, their hair. Pick a reason.

Now add the fact that the Beatles were together fewer than ten years. That's a ridiculously short period of time. I have *underwear* older than that! (Oh, stop looking at me that way...I'll bet you do too.)

So, given all that, why on earth would I choose to write a business book based on the Beatles?

Because business is about success, that's why. This book is about success. *Your* success. And while you can argue all you want to about their music, you can't argue about the Beatles' success. Simply put, when it comes to success, *the Beatles are the gold standard.*

The gold standard. It's a sign of greatness. My favorite definition of greatness is, "When everything that came before you becomes obsolete, and everything that comes after you bears your mark." That definition certainly applies to the Beatles. Wouldn't you like it to apply to your business as well? Perhaps the Fab Four can provide some clues about how to get there.

Why is it that any musical group of note invariably gets compared to the Beatles—and the Beatles invariably come out ahead? It's because the Beatles *are* the gold standard. They define success in their industry (and their insights will help you do the same in yours!). In fact, they are *still*—decades after their break-up—a force to be reckoned with. If you want to know what a lasting success story is all about, think about this. The Beatles broke up in 1970…

- In 1995, in *Forbes* annual listing of the world's highest earning entertainers, the Beatles came in 3rd…after only Steven Spielberg and Oprah Winfrey.
- In 1996, they did the *very same thing again* (although Steven and Oprah changed places). And then they did it again, five years later.
- In 2001, the biggest selling CD in the world—for the year—was the *1* CD…by the Beatles.
- In 2002, in a study by the *Sunday London Times* of British companies with the fastest growing profits, the Beatles' company—Apple Corps. —came in first, with an annual growth rate of *194%*.
- In 2006, the biggest selling CD in the world—for the year—was the *Love* CD…by the Beatles.

With a legacy like that, the question really isn't "Why a business book about the Beatles?" The question is, "Why hasn't there been one until now?"

Because, really now, wouldn't you like *your* organization to be known as the "Beatles" of *your* industry?

THE TOP OF THE CHARTS

The subtitle of this book is *A Handbook for "Top of the Charts" Success*. So let's define what I mean by "top of the charts." And to do that, let's start out by defining what I *don't* mean. I don't mean the "one-hit wonders" or "flashes in the pan" who occasionally hit the top for a nanosecond, and then vanish just as quickly. This book is not titled *The 5 Best Decisions Zagar and Evans Ever Made*. (Who are Zagar and Evans? Exactly!)

I don't mean *hitting* the top of the charts; I mean *dominating* the top of the charts. And what does *dominating* the top of the charts mean? Let's go back to the week of April 4, 1964. The Beatles had the number one song on the charts, *Can't Buy Me Love*. But they also had the number two song on the charts. And the number three song. And number four. And number five. The top five songs in America were all by the Beatles. Nobody else had ever done this before, and nobody else has done it since.

Oh, by the way—that same week, the Beatles also had another seven records in the top 100. As well as the top two albums in the *Billboard* albums chart. And the number one record in the British singles chart, the top two positions in the British albums chart, and the number one position in the British EP chart (The EP was a four-song "mini album" format that never caught on in the States). This is the most complete domination of the British and American charts in history. This is what I mean by "top of the charts" success.

A WORD ABOUT GENIUS

Right now you may be thinking, "Well, yeah...but the Beatles were geniuses." Okay, there's no way around this one. The Beatles—particularly John Lennon and Paul

McCartney—*were* geniuses at songwriting. In fact, Lennon and McCartney are the most successful songwriting team in history. This, of course, leaves me in somewhat of a dilemma, because you can't really begin a book called *The 5 Best Decisions the Beatles Ever Made* with "Decision #1: Be a Genius." It's a nice idea, but it doesn't really work in the real world. The Beatles were also incredibly lucky in their timing, hitting the U.S. just months after the Kennedy assassination, when America's youth were hungry for a new icon. And you can't really follow "Decision #1: Be a Genius" with "Decision #2: Be Incredibly Lucky." If those were the answers to success, this wouldn't be a book—it would be a pamphlet. But fortunately for the rest of us, genius and luck alone are no guarantee of—nor are they requirements for—success. Mensa, the society of geniuses, has more than their fair share of members who are struggling to get by. And luck? How many lottery winners do you know who have gone on to change the world?

The truth is that these four guys—John, Paul, George, and Ringo—did something right. Because success like theirs is not just a function of luck, genius, or any other intangible. Success like theirs is a function of *decisions*—conscious decisions that lead inevitably to the kind of success you and I would both like to achieve.

The rest of this book is about five of these decisions; what I call the Five Best Decisions The Beatles Ever Made. These decisions worked for the Beatles, and they will work for you. If you truly embrace these decisions and make them your own, you'll be well on your way to enjoying the kind of success the Beatles have enjoyed ever since that historic Sunday night. You'll be well on your way to the "top of the charts!"

The 5 Best Decisions

THE BEATLES

Ever Made...

Spread the Spotlight

Decision #1: Spread the Spotlight

"The fact is we were a team, despite everything that went on between us and around us."

\- Paul McCartney

July 6, 1957. It's a warm and humid Saturday afternoon in the seaport town of Liverpool, England. There's a neighborhood party going on (the "annual fete") at a church called St. Peter's, and at this party, a fledgling musical group is bravely plowing through their small repertoire. Their leader: a cocky, sarcastic—and on this particular day, somewhat drunk—16-year old named John Winston Lennon. And this was his band—The Quarry Men.

The Quarry Men played two sets that day: one in the afternoon, one in the evening. Among the audience members were two young boys, Ivan and James. During the break between sets, Ivan—who sometimes played tea-chest bass with The Quarry Men—introduced John Lennon to his 15-year old friend, James. James, who went by his middle name: Paul. Last name, McCartney. Perhaps you've heard of him.

July 6, 1957. The day John Lennon met Paul McCartney. They were together fewer than twenty minutes, and spoke barely five sentences to each other, but it changed everything. Because on that day, John Lennon had a decision to make. It would turn out to be the most important decision of his career.

See, Paul was a rock and roll fan himself, and he'd brought his guitar with him. At a few minutes before 7pm, he picked it up and launched into an Eddie Cochran tune called *Twenty Flight Rock*. And John Lennon quickly found out that not only was this McCartney fellow a better guitar player than he was, but he was also a better singer (at least at the time). Plus, we're talking about Paul McCartney here. "The Cute One." Yep, he was better looking! That's a triple-threat! And so 16-year old John Lennon had a decision to make.

And the decision was this:

"Do I keep the spotlight focused solely on me, as the star of The Quarry Men...or do I *spread the spotlight*, invite this McCartney fellow to join the group, and make the band better, make the *team* stronger?"

Let's put some perspective on this decision, shall we? If you're a man, I want you to think back to when you were 16 years old. Are you there yet? Okay, as a 16-year old adolescent, do you remember what kinds of thoughts were consuming *your entire brain, all the time?* And I mean your *entire* brain: the right half, the creative one, trying to imagine what it will be like when it happens; the left half, the logical one, trying to devise a way to *make* it happen in the first place!

By the way, for you women reading this—if you go back to when *you* were 16...I know *you* know what was on the guys' minds!

Still is, on occasion. Any occasion will do. Arbor Day...supermarket openings...your third cousin's second wife's birthday. The point is, as a 16-year old boy, you're basically hormones with tennis shoes.

Well, it turns out biology is no different on the other side of the Atlantic, and John Lennon was a healthy, red-blooded 16-year-old boy. Not only that, but he was the leader of his own rock and roll band. That's a pretty powerful combination! The last thing you want in this situation is competition. And so if you're John Lennon, the *easy* decision—and the one that many of us probably would have made—would have been to put as much distance between yourself and this McCartney triple-threat as possible.

But we all know what decision 16-year-old John Lennon made. He made the decision to *spread the spotlight*. And the day he made that decision, the Beatles were born. They wouldn't be *called* the Beatles for another few name changes and another few personnel changes, but that core team of Lennon and McCartney was born on that day in Liverpool. And all because 16-

year old John Lennon made the decision to *spread the spotlight*.

Spreading the spotlight. It means making the *team* the star by bringing in diverse talents and sharing the credit. And that's the decision young John Lennon made in the summer of 1957.

At age 16, John Lennon understood something that many people never really get: When you spread the spotlight, everything gets brighter. When you spread the spotlight, you get better results.

ILLUMINATION IS A BRIGHT IDEA

Why do you think the songs of the Beatles are, generally speaking, better than the solo songs of Lennon and McCartney as individuals? (There are exceptions, of course—Lennon's *Imagine* and McCartney's *Band on the Run* come to mind—but we're talking about a rule of thumb here.) It's because John and Paul (and, to a lesser extent, George and Ringo), acting as a team, tended to "filter out" the excesses of each other. On its own, for example, John's music could be a little biting, while Paul's could be a little cutesy. Acting as a team, though, the Beatles could find that perfect balance that created so many hits. When the Beatles split up, and the four started their solo careers, there was no one there to act as the balancer. *Spreading the spotlight* works!

BUT I DON'T *WANT* TO SPREAD THE SPOTLIGHT

Oh, sure...you'd never say that *out loud*. But, from time to time, we all think it. There are times when we just don't want to spread the spotlight. There are times when we just don't want to share the credit. Times like:

- When we're trying to impress the boss
- When we're trying to impress a co-worker
- When we're trying to impress the cute new sales intern

For whatever reason, there are times when we like to keep the credit, the spotlight, all to ourselves. At these times, we should remember what former President Harry S Truman said:

"It's amazing what you can accomplish *if you don't care who gets the credit.*"

Sure, we all have egos, and we all like to be recognized for our accomplishments. That's only human. But when we find ourselves *sabotaging our own long-term success* for the sake of a few short-term pats on the back, there's something wrong. In general, people work better, and produce better results, as a team.

"It's amazing what you can accomplish *if you don't care who gets the credit.*"
- Harry S Truman

I was in Asia recently, speaking to employees of a large Singapore-based media corporation. At one point, one of the attendees—a well-known radio personality—asked, "What can you do when you're part of an on-air radio team, and the team just isn't clicking?"

I'd never been asked that question before, and I was momentarily stumped. So I asked some questions. After a bit of digging, I found out that each member of the team wanted to be the star. Each member of the team wanted *all* the good interviews, *all* the best lines. Not exactly *spreading the spotlight*.

I suggested they try an experiment. I suggested that for *one day*, they make it their sole mission to make the other person the star. Stop interrupting their stories. Set them up for the great punch lines. Just for one day.

A couple of weeks later, when I was back home in the United States, I got an e-mail from the individual who had asked me that question. She told me that she and the other person had decided to give my suggestion a try. And, to be honest, the results weren't that great…the first day. Old habits die hard. But they stuck with it, and within a week, the team—and the show—was clicking. It was funnier, more energetic, and more fun for everybody. And here's the kicker: each member of the team was getting more recognition, and more positive feedback, than they had been when they were trying to be the star. When you spread the spotlight, everything gets brighter.

So put your ego aside for a moment. Let your *team* be the star. Welcome those diverse talents and share the credit. After all, it was Andrew Carnegie who said, "No man will make a great leader who wants to do it all himself or get all the credit for doing it." Credit and recognition are not finite resources; there are plenty of each to go around.

WHY MEN DON'T ASK FOR DIRECTIONS

When John Lennon asked Paul McCartney to join the band, he was acknowledging his willingness to spread the spotlight, to share the credit. (In fact, John and Paul shared the credit in a very literal sense: every song that either of them wrote for the Beatles while the band was together was credited to "Lennon/McCartney," regardless of who actually authored the song.)

But John was doing more than just sharing the credit. He was doing something that many people find much more difficult: he was asking for help. He was, in essence, saying, "I can't do it all by myself. I need somebody with your skill set to make the team better."

For many people—especially people who are good at what they do—it can be real difficult to admit that we could use some help. And let's be honest—it's my gender that has the biggest problem with this. It's the guys. At the risk of over generalizing, women don't tend to make a big deal about this. Women just grasp the concept more easily. It probably goes back to the caveman days, when the men would go out to kill stuff, and the women would stay in the caves bonding socially. (Sample dialog: "You think *you* have it bad? My Thog is such a Neanderthal; if the toilet were invented, he'd never put the seat down.")

The point is (and again, I'm generalizing), guys don't ask for help. Guys don't ask for directions. Guys don't ask for medical assistance. A guy's head could be on fire, and the only thing he's going to ask for is another beer. We men just don't want to admit to what we foolishly perceive as a weakness. Otherwise, the tribe may just kill *us* for dinner, instead of that tasty mammoth.

Sometimes people who are highly accomplished at what they do have difficulty asking for help. They think, "I can do it better by myself." Now granted, there are times when this may in fact be true. But much of the time it's just ego talking. We don't like to admit that we could use help. Sometimes we're not secure enough with our own abilities or leadership to welcome somebody who may have a stronger skill set than we do. We think, consciously or not, that they might threaten our authority. We'll come up with other, more palatable, reasons of course; but at the core, it's a fear of losing control. A true leader, however, knows that the surest way to achieve results is by building the best team possible, by not caring who gets the credit—in short, by spreading the spotlight.

Author Norman Shidle put it particularly well when he said, "A group becomes a team when each member is sure enough of himself and his contributions to praise the skills of the others." A true leader is confident enough to break the "I can do it all myself" mentality.

Truth be told, we *can't* always do it all ourselves. Nor should we want to. (And for all of you multi-talented control freaks out there, just keep repeating this sentence: "Just because I *can* do it all myself doesn't mean I *should*.") Can you imagine the loss to the world (and not just the world of music) had John Lennon let his inner caveman get the better of him?

> *"A group becomes a team when each member is sure enough of himself and his contributions to praise the skills of the others."*
>
> \- Norman Shidle

David Ogilvy, who built one of the most successful advertising agencies in history, once said, "If each of us hires people who are smaller than we are, we shall become a company of dwarfs. But if each of us hires people who are bigger than we are, we shall become a company of giants."

I was speaking recently at a convention in Las Vegas, and afterwards one of the attendees, who worked for a somewhat successful software company, told me this story:

"I'd been an employee of Microsoft for a grand total of one month. I'd arrived at the company with a Masters degree in Math and Computer Science, straight A's, and head full of cockiness. I joined this team that was smart, funny, hungry, friendly, and I worked harder than ever. I quickly got an attitude adjustment after realizing that almost everyone there was super smart. Suffice it to say that the level of expertise was rather intimidating.

"So when I was asked to be on a team interviewing a potential new hire less than four weeks after joining the team myself, I was quite taken aback: 'Wow, I get a say in who gets into Microsoft?!' The interviewee was impressive…very impressive…actually, *too* impressive; his breadth and depth of knowledge were beyond mine! Here I was, barely keeping my head above water in my new job, wondering when I was going to be fired for incompetence, and up pops this new kid whose presence on my team would surely guarantee and hasten my termination. There was no way I was going to let that happen....

"As the interview process progressed, I watched the feedback e-mail coming in. It was clear that the other interviewers realized this guy was brilliant too. Instead of being intimidated by this whippersnapper, however, the other interviewers were giddy with excitement! Oh, the technologies he could 'own;' oh, the projects he could work on...on and on. (This didn't help the sinking feeling in my stomach.)

"This was scary and confusing for me—but then I had a breakthrough. I realized that my awesome team was constantly raising the average smarts of the *entire* team. This doesn't happen by accident. We hired that star—he went on to do very well at Microsoft—and I vowed never to hire anyone who wasn't smarter than I was. This crucial lesson has helped me build two amazing teams that have achieved success beyond the breadth and depth of my own visions."

When you spread the spotlight by hiring people smarter than you, you'll find that they challenge you to be better, they come up with ideas and solutions that constantly surprise you, and your outcomes will be much more successful than they would have been otherwise.

I used to work in the television business. For 15 years, I was the producer of a Seattle-based sketch comedy show called *Almost Live!* I was also a writer and performer for the show, which was number one in its time slot each week of its final ten years on the air. I was a pretty good comedy writer, and an adequate performer, but "pretty good" and "adequate" aren't going to take you to number one. I'm absolutely convinced that the key to *Almost Live's* success—the reason we were number one—was that I hired people who were better than me. I hired better actors, and I hired better writers. Yes, on occasion my ego took a bit of a beating. This generally happened during what we called a "pitch meeting."

A pitch meeting is a vile, odious thing which is to egos what a paper shredder is to paper. The purpose of these meetings is to determine whose ideas will make it onto the show that week. During our pitch meetings, we'd all gather around a big round table and read the material we'd been working on. This can be a very intimidating experience…particularly when everybody else's stuff is getting bigger laughs than yours! Oh, occasionally my stuff would hold its own, but generally the big laughs went to the others. And we were number one for ten straight years.

The smartest thing I ever did was hire people who were better than me.

THE MYTH OF THE LONE RANGER

Americans have a fascination with the Lone Ranger. Not necessarily the Old West character played by Clayton Moore in the 1950s, but rather the whole idea of one man or woman acting alone, and triumphing against the odds. It's a romantic idea; one that has driven countless movies starring Gary Cooper, Clint Eastwood, and

Harrison Ford (and, to a lesser extent, Jerry Lewis).

But it's a myth.

In the real world, the biggest accomplishments tend to be the result of a team working together toward a common goal. Why is this? It's because when it comes to solving problems, tackling projects, and achieving goals, a team offers substantial advantages over an individual. Among other things, a team provides:

- Greater quantity of ideas
- Greater diversity of ideas
- Deeper base of experience
- Greater chance of one idea sparking another
- More impartial evaluation of ideas

In his groundbreaking book, *The Wisdom of Crowds*, James Surowiecki makes the case that groups of people, in general, are better than individuals or an elite few at things like solving problems, fostering innovation, coming to wise decisions, even predicting the future. "It's as if," Surowiecki says, "we've been programmed to be collectively smart."

Yes, an individual acting alone can accomplish great things. But the odds are better with a team. A study published by the American Psychological Association in April, 2006 verifies that teams perform better on complex problem solving than the best of an equivalent number of individuals working alone. And this is just one of many studies that have shown the same result: in general, teams perform better than individuals.

And yet the myth persists. It persists because it's fun. It's fun to imagine being the hero in the black mask, riding off into the sunset while the townspeople ask, "Who was that masked man?" But it's still a myth. After all, even the Lone Ranger had Tonto.

A VERY SIMPLE QUESTION

Spreading the spotlight means making the *team* the star by bringing in diverse talents and sharing the credit. John Lennon, who could have easily kept the spotlight all to himself, brought in Paul McCartney. Paul McCartney, in turn, introduced John to George Harrison. With the addition of Ringo Starr, the chemistry was complete. Spreading the spotlight clearly worked for the Beatles. But some people need convincing.

So if you know somebody who doesn't seem to grasp this whole *spreading the spotlight* concept; if you know someone who isn't interested in sharing the credit; if you know someone who is genetically incapable of asking for help…then I encourage you to tell him or her the story of 16-year-old John Lennon. Because, ultimately, the question is a very simple one. When you think about yourself, and your relationship with your team, the question is a very simple one:

Would you rather be the *star* of the Quarry Men…or a *member* of the Beatles?

"Top of the Charts" Challenge

It's one thing to read about the 5 Decisions that led to the Beatles' success, but it's another thing to truly make them your own. That's why each of the 5 Decisions will be followed by a "Top of the Charts" Challenge section. Each of these sections will have questions and exercises that will help you to anchor the preceding Decision to your own situation and your own team.

These Challenge sections are intended to be used as mini-workbooks. That means it's okay (encouraged, even) to write in the book! The questions are designed to challenge your thinking about how each Decision applies to you, and the space following each question is for you to record your thoughts. To get started, turn the page.

1. What would Spreading the Spotlight look like with my team, and how would it benefit us?

2. How could we be greater if we Spread the Spotlight?

3. Where have I not been willing to share the credit...and why?

4. Who on my team makes me play at a higher level?

5. Whom on my team do I inspire to play at a higher level?

The 5 Best Decisions
THE BEATLES
Ever Made...

A Single, Shared Vision

Decision #2: A Single, Shared Vision

"Where are we going, fellas?"

\- John Lennon

When the Beatles were first starting out—well before they were even called the Beatles—there were over 300 other rock and roll bands. Not in the world. Not even in England. In Liverpool alone. Over 300 other rock and roll bands...and most of them were better than the Beatles.

So how did the Beatles manage to rise to the top of the charts? There were certainly a number of different elements, but the one that drove all the others was this one:

The Beatles had a single, shared vision.

A single, shared vision. And it was this: They were going to be bigger than Elvis!

Now, you have to understand something. Back in those heady days of the late 50s and early 60s, Elvis Presley was the biggest there was, the biggest there ever had been, the biggest there ever *would* be. And the Beatles were going to be bigger.

They knew *exactly* where they were going. In the very early days as a matter of fact, whenever the band was feeling down—they didn't have any money, nobody would book them, they couldn't get a recording contract—*whenever* they were feeling down, their leader, John Lennon, would suddenly shout out, "Where are we going?"

And they'd all shout back, "To the top, Johnny!"

"Where's that, fellas?"

"To the toppermost of the poppermost!"

A little hokey? A little corny? Maybe. But the point is this: They all said the same thing. They all had that *single, shared vision*. And that, more than virtually anything else, is what drove them to the top. (Conversely, it was when they started to *lose* that single, shared vision that they began the internal descent that would eventually lead to their breakup.)

"Bigger than Elvis," "the toppermost of the poppermost," became the yardstick against which they measured all their other decisions. With every ensuing decision the Beatles made—what songs to record, what outfits to wear, what venues to play—the question, either conscious or subconscious, was, "Is this taking us closer to, or farther away from, our single, shared vision?"

MY EMBARRASSING CONFESSION

Okay, it's "embarrassing confession" time.

From the age of sixteen to the age of eighteen, I was the drummer for the powerhouse, Top 40 rock and roll band...Liptastic.

Yes, you read that correctly. And the really sad thing is that it took us three days to come up with that name.

Liptastic was a powerhouse, Top 40 rock and roll band in my hometown of Lancaster, Pennsylvania. Home of the Pennsylvania Dutch.

The Amish.

Not exactly known for their rock and roll heritage. More into quilting, really. The point is that Lancaster, Pennsylvania was not what you might call a rock and roll "hotbed." There were not 300 other rock and roll bands in Lancaster. There were maybe 8. And, of those 8, Liptastic was ranked 17th. We *never* thought we were going to be bigger than Elvis. Our *single, shared vision* was to play our set list as quickly as possible and go home. Not exactly a ticket to greatness.

But over in England, the Beatles *had* that single, shared vision. And it propelled them to the top of the charts.

Now, did having that single, shared vision, in and of itself, guarantee the Beatles' success? Of course not. It took luck, timing, talent—the alignment of a hundred different elements. But if the Beatles hadn't had that single, shared vision *first*, none of the rest of it would have ever happened.

IF YOU CAN'T SAY IT, IT AIN'T THERE

"But Bill," you say, "I don't need a single, shared vision. I have a pretty good general idea of where I want to go, and my team knows basically where we're heading."

Let me put it this way: If you're a ship captain, I don't want to be on that cruise!

Look, if you really want to get to the top of the charts, a wishy-washy attitude like that is just not going to cut it. If you can't *articulate* your vision, you don't *have* a vision. Articulating your vision gives it definition and focus. There's a sense of clarity that comes with having a clearly defined vision. It becomes the litmus test against which all other decisions are made. Any time a decision comes up, you can first ask this question: "Will this take me closer to, or farther away from, my vision?" It's amazing how many decisions practically make themselves when put honestly to that test.

It's been well documented that most business fail within the first five years. The primary reason for this is lack of adequate start-up capital, but another significant reason is the lack of a clearly articulated vision. "Being successful," or "Making lots of money" won't do it. They're too general and ill-defined. A good single, shared vision is one that encompasses your entire endeavor, but is still concrete enough to track.

When you can articulate it, you can achieve it.

KEEP IT *SIMPLE*

Now the thing of it is, the Beatles' vision—"bigger than Elvis"—is not a complicated one. They didn't bring in a team of consultants and run DISC assessments to come up with it. None of the four Beatles labeled it a "Mission Statement," framed it, and hung it in a lunchroom.

They *lived* it.

The point is, your single, shared vision doesn't have to be complicated. It doesn't have to be a paragraph long. It doesn't have to be printed on vellum in Olde English script.

What it *does* have to be...is simple.

Notice I said "simple," *not* "simplistic." "Bigger than Elvis" is simple. It's clear, it's understandable, and it doesn't require extensive memorization. And it drives every other decision.

In their book, *Made to Stick: Why Some Ideas Survive and Others Die*, authors Chip and Dan Heath define "simple" as *finding the core of the idea*. This means stripping the idea, the vision, down to its most critical essence. For the Beatles, "Bigger than Elvis" was the critical essence; it provided the destination. And, as the Heaths point out, "When people know the desired destination, they're free to improvise, as needed, in arriving there.... As soon as people know what the *intent* is they begin generating their own solutions."

ANOTHER MINOR SUCCESS STORY

Some years ago a fellow named Bill Gates had a company called Microsoft. He had a single, shared vision for his company, and it was this:

A computer on every desk.

Talk about simple! And that single, shared vision drove everything else that Bill Gates and Microsoft did. I understand it worked out pretty well for them.

The beauty of a simple vision is that it can be all encompassing. Something like, "Sell 42% more widgets this year" won't work. It's a fine *goal*, but a lousy *vision*. It can help you with widget decisions, but not much else. A simple, all encompassing vision, however, can drive an entire organization forward. It becomes a litmus test for everything else you do.

But, like a good goal, it must also be measurable. "Bigger than Elvis." "A computer on every desk." "A man on the moon by the end of the decade." These are big statements; statements that inspire the emotions. That's vital. But they are also measurable. Again, "Is this decision getting us closer to, or farther away from, our single, shared vision?" When that vision is measurable, you'll always know.

"20 VISION" SYNDROME

For some people, the problem isn't creating a single, shared vision. The problem is creating just *one* single, shared vision. Some people simply have too many visions! You probably know people like this (perhaps you even *are* one): ideas tumble out of their heads like the popcorn in a movie theater popping machine. They keep coming and coming until the brain, in desperation, finally screams out:

"TOO MANY OPTIONS!"

At which point, it simply freezes up. When we're confronted with too many choices, we go into a sort of paralysis. (If you don't believe me, try shopping for mustard at a gourmet food store.) And so, despite the wealth of good ideas, nothing gets done. So the ideas are not the problem. The problem is a lack of direction, a lack of focus. There's plenty of gas in the car, but no road map. An overarching single, shared vision provides this road map.

If ever there was brain that had no shortage of ideas, it was the one belonging to Leonardo da Vinci. Artist, architect, scientist—he began hundreds of projects in dozens of arenas. And yet he completed very few. In fact, one of his biggest regrets as he lay on his deathbed was that he had left so much work uncompleted. Ideas are not the problem.

Certainly, the Beatles had many ideas and many decisions to make. What songs should we play? What venues should we play? What offers should we accept? What clothes should we wear? But what kept the Beatles moving forward, rather than stalling in their tracks, was that each of these decisions, consciously or unconsciously, was weighed against their single, shared vision: Will this take us closer to, or farther away from, being bigger than Elvis? Which decisions will take us to the toppermost of the poppermost?

YOU CAN'T ASSIGN A SHARED VISION

I once worked for a man who considered himself a visionary leader. With a gleam in his eye, he would gather the team into his office and reveal "the grand vision." He'd tell us that his vision was our vision, and then expect us to go out and make it happen.

There were only two problems.

First, this was practically a monthly occurrence, and the vision was always different. He'd read a new business book, or a new magazine article, or a new fortune cookie, and all of a sudden the old vision was out and we'd be assigned a new one. This is called "Flavor-of-the-Month Management," and it's generally less than effective.

The second problem was that we all hated his ideas! Okay, "hated" is a pretty strong word. Perhaps a better word would be "loathed." Or "abhorred." Maybe "detested." The point is that we didn't buy into his vision. And needless to say, the results mirrored our efforts (more on this in chapter 5).

In short, my boss had a *single* vision (at least until the next book/article/fortune cookie came out), but it wasn't a *shared* vision. You can't assign a shared vision. To "share" means to "possess a view or quality in common with others." It's that "in common" part that my boss didn't quite grasp. He didn't understand that for a team to embrace a vision, they must first "buy in" to that vision. They have to make it *theirs*. That's not going to happen if the vision doesn't excite the emotions, and it's not going to happen if the members of the team don't have a clear concept of their role in the vision.

ALL TOGETHER NOW

So how do you get this kind of "buy-in" from your team? Well, the easiest way is to simply hire people who already share your vision. Each of the early hires at Microsoft shared Bill Gates's vision of "a computer on every desk." They were excited by it, and they worked diligently to make it a reality. The more well defined your vision is, the more you'll start attracting applicants who already support that vision. People want to work for companies like Ben & Jerry's and Starbucks not just for the paycheck, but because they believe in the vision.

We don't always have the luxury, though, of creating our perfect team from scratch, do we? (Answer: no.) Sometimes, maybe even most times, the team is already in place. It's our job as a leader to get that elusive "buy-in" from people who may have some degree of resistance. In a case like this, dictating the "shared vision" is the worst possible course of action. It will only increase the resistance. (After all, don't *you* tend to resist things that are forced upon you?) Instead, you'll find it far more productive to give these people a sense of ownership in the vision. That doesn't necessarily mean letting them decide what the vision is. What it *does* mean is asking them questions like:

- How can we best implement this vision?

- In what ways can you and your department help make this vision succeed?
- When the vision is achieved, how will you benefit?
- What are some ways we can get "buy-in" from others for this vision?
- What will the achievement of this vision look like for you?

Questions like these promote that sense of ownership in the vision that is so crucial to getting "buy-in." Once your team members start seeing themselves and their roles as a part of the vision (as opposed to "apart *from* the vision"), the vision itself becomes a shared one.

WHAT ABOUT YOU?

So what's *your* single, shared vision? What is it that will drive you, your team, and your organization to the "toppermost of the poppermost"?

What is it that will excite, inspire, and energize your team to reach that goal? What is it that will fire the emotions of everybody on your team?

Big questions? Yep. Difficult questions? You bet! Impossible questions? Not for the people who achieve unusual success.

So I want you to imagine that you're with your team right now. If you were to suddenly shout out, "Where are we going?" (and by the way, I don't suggest that you actually do this; your team will think that either you've gone crazy, or worse, you've read a business book)—would they all say the same thing? Do they have that *single, shared vision*?

"Where are we going?"

When I ask that question during my keynote presentations, I'm always interested to see the response from the audience. Many people seem to take this question as a cue to look down at their feet. But the ones who are nodding "yes" are looking me right in the eye...and they're smiling. They're the ones who are well on their way to turning that single, shared vision into reality.

I've been in both places, and I can tell you from experience that it's more fun in the second group. And it all begins with a single, shared vision. What's yours?

"Top of the Charts" Challenge

1. What vision do I have for myself? For my team?

SEAMLESS SUPPORT FOR SUPERIOR SUCESS

SUCCESS MEASURED THROUGH THE EYES OF OTHERS (OUR CUSTOMERS)

SUCESS THROUGH SUPERIOR SEAMLESS SUPPORT

2. Is my vision:

    - simple enough to be easily remembered?
    - broad enough to be all-encompassing?
    - inspiring enough to fuel the emotions?

3. How does my vision fit in with the company or organizational vision?

4. How can we best implement this vision?

5. In what ways can my team and I help make this vision succeed?

6. When the vision is achieved, how will my team and I benefit?

7. What are some ways that I can get "buy-in" for my vision?

8. What will the achievement of this vision look like?

The 5 Best Decisions THE BEATLES Ever Made...

Play to Your Strengths

Decision #3: Play to Your Strengths

"We'd be on the tour bus, and Roy Orbison was on the back of the bus, and he played us 'Pretty Woman,' and we'd think, 'We've gotta write one as good as that!' We were trying to improve all the time."

-Paul McCartney

The Beatles' first single was a song called *Love Me Do*. When it was originally released, it went to number seventeen in the British charts. That's a pretty respectable debut for a brand new band. But "respectable" doesn't get you to the "toppermost of the poppermost." It doesn't get you "bigger than Elvis."

The Beatles felt that they could do better.

And, more importantly (at least at this point), so did their producer, George Martin. Martin had been in the business a long time, and had a good set of ears. So when it came time for the Beatles to record their second single, Martin acquired for them a professionally written song called *How Do You Do It*. To his ears, this sounded like a hit record. This was exciting news! Martin's fledgling band, the Beatles, might have a shot at number one with this song!

But when he offered it to the Beatles, they turned it down.

Out of respect for their experienced producer, though, the Beatles *did* record a demo of the song. Martin then gave this demo to another band he was producing—Gerry and the Pacemakers—and told them to play it *just like the Beatles' version*. Gerry and the boys did just that…and their version went to number 1!

It was a hit record—a sure thing—and the Beatles turned it down. Now, why would they do that?

They turned it down because of their third decision: the decision to *play to their strengths*. And to the Beatles, this meant their strengths as songwriters. They wanted all of their singles to be *Beatles originals*. (In those days, singles were the important recordings; albums were more of an afterthought.) Even at this early stage, the Beatles were thinking long-term, rather than "one hit wonder."

So the Beatles passed on *How Do You Do It*, and instead recorded a John Lennon composition called *Please Please Me*. It went to number one in most of the British charts.

The Beatles realized that if they were really going to be "bigger than Elvis," they couldn't be just another cookie-cutter band playing cookie-cutter songs. They had to be different. They had to be unique. In other words, they had to answer the question that most of us never even ask:

"What is it that we can do better than anyone else?"

In other words, what is our biggest *strength?*

It's amazing, but most of us go through our entire lives without ever asking—much less answering—that question. "What is it that we can do better than anyone else?" When you can answer that question, *and stay focused on the answer*, your success is virtually guaranteed. But you have to stay focused! It's easy to stray off course.

What is it that you can do better than anyone else?

ALMOST LIVE! STRAYS OFF COURSE

As I mentioned in chapter one, I was for fifteen years the producer of a Seattle-based sketch comedy TV show called *Almost Live!* Our job was to make fun of Seattle: its people, its neighborhoods, its customs. That was our strength—and we were really, really good at it. So good, in fact, that people kept telling us, "You guys should go national!" Well, lo and behold, one day the phone rang. It was Comedy Central—the national comedy network. The next thing we knew, we were a *national* sketch comedy show! And we were really, really...average...at it. Don't get me wrong—we were okay. But just okay. It wasn't our strength. So at the end of the two and a half year contract, we opted not to renew (and by "we" I mean "Comedy Central"). We went back to doing what we did best. And from that point on, we were never less than number one in the ratings, not even for a single week.

When you play to your strengths, you make better music.

THE WRONG SIDE OF THE EQUATION

So often, though, we focus on the other side of the equation. We tend to spend an inordinate amount of time focusing on our *weaknesses*. The thought process seems to be:

"My strengths will take care of themselves; I really don't need to worry about them. Instead, I'm going to spend the bulk of my time trying to improve my weaknesses, so that they, too, can become strengths."

It's a nice theory, and it sells a lot of self-help books, but it usually doesn't work in the real world. What happens instead is that, while the weaknesses *do* improve a bit (although generally not to the level where we can honestly call them strengths), the strengths—because of lack of attention—begin to atrophy, to diminish. And soon we find ourselves in this middle ground, which is called *average*.

Business guru Peter Drucker famously outlined what he called "The Five Deadly Business Sins." One of these sins was "feeding problems and starving opportunities." Drucker found that in virtually all the businesses he worked with, the best performing people were assigned to problems, while the opportunities were left to fend for themselves. And yet, as he points out, only opportunities produce results and growth. Imagine how much better these businesses would be if they allocated their best resources to those areas that produce results and growth.

To paraphrase Drucker, focusing on our strengths moves us forward. Focusing on our weaknesses keeps us mired in the past.

A TELLING QUESTION

Not long ago, The Gallup Organization conducted a survey of nearly 200,000 employees in nearly 8,000 business units within 36 companies. Among other questions, the employees were asked this one:

At work, do you have the opportunity to do what you do best every day?

Before I give you the results of that survey, I want you to think about that question for yourself.

At work, do you have the opportunity to do *what you do best* every day?

If you're like 80 percent of the people surveyed, your answer is no. *80 percent!* What that means, of course, is that only *20 percent of employees feel they are "playing to their strengths" every day.*

What makes this particularly distressing is that those employees who *were* able to answer "yes" were more likely to:

- work in business units with lower employee turnover,
- work in more productive business units, and
- work in business units with higher customer satisfaction scores.

(Incidentally, Gallup has subsequently asked this question of more than 1.7 million employees in 101 companies from 63 countries—with the same results.)

At work, do you have the opportunity to do what you do best every day?

The conclusion is clear: When you play to your strengths, you get better results!

Most organizations, though, take their employees' strengths for granted and focus instead on minimizing, i.e., fixing, their weaknesses. (If you don't believe me, think back to the last time you gave or received "The Dreaded Performance Review." Where was most of the time focused: on strengths or on weaknesses? I rest my case.) Now why, given the above research, would they do that? Marcus Buckingham, author of *First, Break All the Rules* and *Now, Discover Your Strengths*, believes it's because most organizations are built on a flawed assumption about people.

Most organizations, Buckingham says, operate on the assumption that a person's greatest room for growth is in his or her areas of greatest weakness. But the best organizations realize that just the opposite is true:

Our greatest room for growth is in the areas of our greatest strengths!

WHAT'S YOUR INSTRUMENT?

Within the Beatles, George Harrison was the lead guitarist. That's what he did best. The Beatles didn't waste a lot of time working with George on his weak drumming skills. Why? Because Ringo was already handling that job brilliantly. Drumming was what *he* did best. Each of the four Beatles *was* able to "play to their strengths"—every day.

(By the way, there are those who will try to tell you that Ringo wasn't really that good a drummer, and that his contributions to the Beatles were negligible. As a lifelong drummer myself, I'm here to tell you that Ringo Starr is one of the greatest rock drummers of all time. Don't believe me? Imagine you're a drummer in the 60s. Most rock and roll drumming is simple, bubblegum stuff. Then somebody—say, John Lennon—starts shaking things up (see chapter 4) by bringing in stuff like *She Said, She Said*; *Strawberry Fields Forever*; and *A Day In The Life*. You then come up with drum parts that are not just *good*, but so astonishingly innovative that it's all but impossible to imagine the songs played any other way. "Yes, but I can play anything Ringo played," the detractors will say. To which I reply, "So can I. I can also sit down at my computer and retype *Hamlet*, but that doesn't make me Shakespeare." I mean, who's the artist here: the guy who copies something note for note, or the guy who came up with it in the first place? Sorry to go off on a rant, but I have to defend my man Ringo. We now return to our regularly scheduled programming.)

When you put together a great team, and then let each team member do what they do best, great things can happen. Sadly, though, many organizations don't seem to get this concept. If the Beatles were a modern company, it wouldn't be too hard to imagine this performance review:

> *Reviewer:* "Ringo, looking over your work for the past year, I see your drumming skills are quite good. However, under 'Areas for Improvement,' your lead guitar work just isn't where we'd like it to be."
>
> *Ringo:* "Well, that's because I'm a drummer, not a lead guitarist."
>
> *Reviewer:* "We think that's a narrow way of looking at things. Here at Beatles, Inc., we feel all our employees should be well-rounded musicians. So for the next 90 days, I'd like you to spend less

> time drumming and instead really work on those lead guitar skills, okay?"
>
> *Ringo:* "I'm not sure that makes sense."
>
> *Reviewer:* "Ringo, you just have to trust us on this. After all, we're management."

Sounds a little ridiculous, doesn't it? And yet you probably know of organizations that are run that way. Perhaps you even work for one.

Look at your own team. Spend a few minutes and take a little "strengths inventory." On a piece of paper, list the members of your team. Then, next to their names, write down what unique abilities each member brings to the table. Is Tom a great "detail person," while Catherine is an outstanding long-range planner? Does Randy have a creative mind that comes up with one idea after another, while Jennifer is particularly skilled at implementation? What are the strengths of your team members?

Once you've established these strengths, take a look at the work you'd like your team to accomplish. How can you best utilize the teams' strengths to accomplish the teams' goals? That's where your focus should be. Find ways to let your team members "play to their strengths" every day.

SO WHAT ABOUT THE DAMN WEAKNESSES?

So does all this mean that you can disregard those areas where you don't shine? Absolutely not. I'm not suggesting that you ignore your weaknesses—just don't *live* there. I'm saying put the majority of your effort into your areas of strength, not into your areas of weakness.

If an area of weakness is something necessary and germane to your work, and you can't assign it, delegate it, or outsource it to anyone else, then you simply must work on it. If, for example, you're an airplane pilot, but you just can't seem to get the hang of that whole "landing" thing...well, you may need to give that a bit of attention (or find another line of work). But if you're honest about it, you'll find that the jobs that fit the above parameters are actually pretty uncommon.

Speaking of airplanes, I live pretty close to where Boeing builds its biggest planes, like the 747. Except that Boeing doesn't really build the planes—it *assembles* them. Most of the components—the seats, the overhead bins, the engines—are made by other suppliers. Boeing's strength is in designing and assembling aircraft, not in building overhead bins. Boeing devotes its energy to doing what it does best, and lets its suppliers do what *they* do best.

WHAT ABOUT YOU?

Since your strengths are unique to you, it's up to you to determine what they are. It's up to you to determine what it is that you do *best*…

- as an individual within a team
- as a team within an organization
- as an organization within an industry.

(By the way, I'm assuming that you're already good at what you do. If you're not good, you really have only two choices: get good…or get out.)

So you're already good. Now, what is it that you can do *better than anyone else?* For the Beatles, the answer was songwriting. They poured the bulk of their energy into this strength. Even when they were the acknowledged masters, the best of the best, they kept striving to improve, to take their strengths to new and higher levels.

Which is why the title of this book is *The 5 Best Decisions The Beatles Ever Made*, and not *The 5 Best Decisions Gerry and the Pacemakers Ever Made*.

"Top of the Charts" Challenge

1. What are the primary strengths of the members of my team?

2. Team exercise: Have each member of your team write down three things they can do that the other team members might be surprised to know (e.g., play the accordian, cook a great omelet, ride a horse). Shuffle all the answers up, and then, reading them one by one, have the team members try to guess which skill belongs to which person. Not only is this a great team-building exercise, but it may reveal traits and abilities that could be useful in current and future projects.

3. What is an issue that my team is working on currently?

4. How can my team's strengths best be allocated to resolving the issue identified in question three?

5. What are some things we're doing now that are not playing to our strengths?

6. How can we change the way we're doing these things to better focus on our strengths?

7. How can I make sure that each member of my team has an opportunity to do what he/she does best every day?

The 5 Best Decisions THE BEATLES Ever Made...

SHAKE IT UP!

Decision #4: Shake It Up!

"They'd say, 'Well, our rule book says...' and we'd say, 'They're out of date, come on, let's move!' We always wanted things to be different because we knew that people, generally, always want to move on, and if we hadn't pushed them, the guys would have stuck by their rule books."

\- Paul McCartney

Shake it up! It means being willing (eager, even) to challenge the rules...to do things differently...to grow...to evolve. It's how you keep the competition on their toes, and how you keep yourself fresh and enthusiastic.

For this, the Beatles' fourth decision, I want to take you back to August 29, 1966. San Francisco. Candlestick Park. The Beatles are playing a concert in front of an enthusiastic crowd of 25,000 screaming fans.

None of those fans knew it at the time—in fact, nobody except the four men on stage knew it—but it would be the last concert the Beatles would ever play.

And they were at the top of their game.

The top of their game, and they decided to call it quits. No more tours. No more concerts. No more live appearances. From that day on, the Beatles would become recording artists *only*.

And the rules said you couldn't do that.

The rules said you *had* to tour. You *had* to get out there with the people. You *had* to support your records with live appearances. To do otherwise was to commit career suicide. And that's what virtually everybody in the music business thought the Beatles had done by making the decision to shake things up and stop touring.

Until June 1, 1967—nearly nine months to the day from that last show in San Francisco.

June 1, 1967. That's the day the Beatles released their new album—a monumental piece of work called *Sgt. Pepper's Lonely Hearts Club Band*. This was an album that shook things up in every way possible: musically, lyrically, visually. It's the album that turned rock and roll into an art form.

And it went to number one.

Without a tour.

See, for the Beatles, the grueling "touring/concerts/live appearances" model no longer worked. They weren't enjoying it, and because the screaming of the fans kept them from actually hearing what they were playing, their musicianship was deteriorating. More importantly, the music they were writing was getting more and more advanced—to the point that it would have been impossible, given the limitations of the day, to perform live.

In other words, "the rules" no longer supported the Beatles' vision. And so they shook things up.

By shaking things up—by letting go of a system that no longer fit the vision—the Beatles were able to take their career to a level that even they couldn't have dreamed of...a level of unsurpassed richness and creativity.

All because they decided to shake things up.

Yes, the Beatles could have kept on touring. They could have kept writing the same kinds of songs. They could have remained the "four moptops." It would have been the easy decision. But have you ever noticed that the easy decision isn't always the right decision? Yes, the Beatles could have kept on touring. It would have been the popular decision. But have you ever noticed that the popular decision isn't always the right decision?

TWO TRAPS

It can take a lot of courage to make the difficult, unpopular decision. It can take a lot of courage to shake things up. People like the status quo. But when we keep doing what we've always been doing—even if we do it better than anyone else—we fall into two traps:

Trap #1: Complacency

When we keep doing something the same way, even if we're good at it (in fact, *especially* if we're good at it), we tend to get a bit complacent about it. We take it for granted. The excitement wears off, and we can find ourselves "phoning it in." When we hit this stage, we lose momentum, and it gets harder and harder to rekindle the fire that brought us to the top in the first place. The Beatles had already entered this stage, and they realized it. Thus, their decision to shake it up.

Trap #2: The Competition

Business is tough these days, and the competition can be fierce. If we keep doing things the same way (again, even if we're good at it), it makes it easier for the competition to catch up to us. And then, if we *keep* doing things the same way...the competition can pass us. By shaking things up and challenging the rules, we can go places the competition can't even imagine.

It's the Niche That'll Kill You

The Swiss are famous for three things: chocolate, pocketknives...and watches. Swiss watches are legendary for their beauty, their accuracy, and their engineering. In 1968, in fact, the Swiss held roughly 80% of the world watch market. Today, they hold less than 10%. What happened? The advent of digital watches: watches that have no hands, don't tick, and rely on electronics instead of springs and gears. Digital watches took the world by storm, and Swiss domination disappeared virtually overnight. But do you know who invented digital watches?

The Swiss.

The Swiss invented the technology behind the digital watch. But the Swiss weren't willing to shake things up. To the Swiss, a watch was something that had hands, ticked, and relied on springs and gears. They refused to embrace—or, even worse, patent—their own technology because of their narrow idea of what a "watch" is. Subsequently, a Japanese company picked up this unprotected technology and ran with it. That company was Seiko.

If we keep doing things the same way (even if we're good at it), it makes it easier for the competition to catch up to us.

Earlier I mentioned Peter Drucker's "Five Deadly Business Sins." The fourth sin is "Slaughtering tomorrow's opportunity on the altar of yesterday." If you stay mired in "the way things are" (which all too quickly becomes "the way things were"—the altar of yesterday), you kill the chance to move ahead (tomorrow's opportunity). And if you don't move ahead, you can bet the competition will.

To the world, the Moptops were a pop band. To the four Beatles, this was too limiting. They didn't want to be stuck in a narrow definition of what a pop band was.

So they shook things up and expanded the realm of "pop" music to include multiple genres: reggae (*Ob-La-Di, Ob-La-Da*), bluegrass (*Rocky Raccoon*), and experimental (*Revolution #9*), to name but a few. Some of these were more successful than others, but the bottom line is: The competition didn't have a chance. How do you catch up to a moving target?

Once they had the first few albums under their belt, the Beatles shook things up with each subsequent release. And each time they shook things up, they were taking a risk. They risked losing a fan base that didn't want them to change. The Beatles were sailing into uncharted waters, and some of the fans didn't want to leave the shore. But every great accomplishment includes risk.

No one would have blamed Columbus if he had turned back. But no one would have remembered him either.

MAKE IT FUN!

One of our finest philosophers, the late, great Katharine Hepburn, once said:

"If you obey all the rules, you miss all the fun!"

Hepburn certainly knew a thing or two about shaking it up and challenging the rules—and about having fun! And that brings up an important point:

Success should *be fun!*

> *"If you obey all the rules, you miss all the fun!"*
> - Katherine Hepburn

Yes, by all means treat your success seriously. But "serious" doesn't mean "somber." The Beatles were *very* serious about their success...and they made sure to have fun along the way.

(Just one example: the last track on the *Sgt. Pepper's Lonely Hearts Club Band* album. Do you know what it is? Even people who are familiar with the album get this one wrong. They generally say *A Day In the Life*—which *is* the last *song*...but it's not the last *track*. The reason most people get this question wrong is because most people can't hear the last track—but their dogs can. That's because the last track on the *Sgt. Pepper's Lonely Hearts Club Band* album is a 15 kilocycle dog whistle that John Lennon recorded as a special message from himself to all the dogs in the world...just for fun!)

When Paul was asked how the four of them had coped with the pressure of Beatlemania, he said, "It didn't seem like pressure. It was, but I don't remember it being a pressure. It was *fun*."

Yes, success should be fun. Find ways to celebrate the successes—the little ones as well as the big ones. When I was speaking to a group of call center professionals, I discovered that they routinely had contests, games, and celebrations. They decorated their workspace with different themes throughout the year. Of course they worked hard. But they knew how to add a touch of humor to the work. The humor, in turn, helped them become more creative (humor and creativity are really two sides of the same coin), which made it easier to "shake it up" and keep things fresh.

Now, clearly there are some work situations where a bit of judgment is in order. If you're an air traffic controller, you probably shouldn't be obscuring your radar screen with happy-face decals. If you're a Supreme Court justice, covering your robe with pink and gold sequins, though fun, might be considered inappropriate. (What you wear *under* your robe is your own business.) The point, though, is that "work" and "fun" are not mutually exclusive terms. You should always be on the lookout for ways to bring them together.

LEGAL DISCLAIMER

In this section, I've talked about shaking things up by challenging the rules. Please note, I'm saying *challenge* the rules. I'm not advocating that you go around *breaking* the rules willy-nilly. That's the kind of strategy that can get you ten to twenty in Leavenworth. Don't shake things up just for the sake of shaking them up. For example, setting fire to your office furniture will shake things up. Deleting all financial records from the company's server will shake things up. Going to work naked will shake things up. In several ways. I'm not advocating that you do any of these things.

What I *am* advocating is that you give yourself permission to look closely at the way you are currently doing things and then ask some questions:

- *Why* am I doing it this way?
- Is there a different way to do this?
- Is there a *better* way to do this?

Give your teams permission to ask these same questions. Give them permission to shake things up. Maybe there *is* a different way. Maybe there *is* a better way. Maybe you can make your *own* Sgt. Pepper.

"Top of the Charts" Challenge

1. What are some of the processes that we do on a routine basis?

2. Why are we doing them the way we do? (It may turn out there are very good reasons; it may turn out that some "shaking up" is in order.)

3. Exercise: Look for simple opportunities to "shake it up" in your everyday life. These simple exercises will help you to break the ingrained patterns in your life, and get your brain thinking more creatively. Some examples are:

    - Try a new route home from work
    - Brush your teeth with your other hand
    - Wear your watch on your other arm for a day
    - Sit in a different seat at the dining table
    - Listen to a new radio station on the way to work

4. Now, transfer these ideas to some of your workplace patterns. For example, do you always have the staff meeting at the same time on the same day? Try "shaking it up"!

5. What are some ways to add an element of fun to what you and your team are doing? How can you celebrate your successes?

The 5 Best Decisions THE BEATLES Ever Made...

CARRY THAT WEIGHT

Decision #5: Carry That Weight

"The reason we were twice as good as anyone else is because we worked twice as hard as anyone else."

- Paul McCartney

Okay, let's be honest here. You can *spread the spotlight* and have a great team; you can develop a *single, shared vision*; you can identify and *play to your strengths*; and you can even *shake it up* a little. But until somebody rolls up their sleeves and does the heavy lifting, nothing is going to happen.

And that's what this final decision is all about: doing the heavy lifting, going the extra mile, doing what it takes...*carrying that weight.*

To illustrate what I mean, let's take a snapshot of the Beatles' career:

- 12 albums, 11 of which went to #1
- 22 singles, 17 of which went to #1
- 4 movies
- 52 BBC radio appearances
- over 1,400 live appearances

And they did virtually *all* of this...in just five years.

Five years! For most bands today, that would mean two albums and two tours.

Remember, the Beatles' first *Ed Sullivan* appearance was on February 9, 1964. The last time all four Beatles were in the studio together was August 20, 1969.

Now, I don't know what *you've* been doing for the past five years. *My* big accomplishment during that time span? I fixed my upstairs toilet. And when I say *I* fixed it, I mean I called a guy, and he came over and took care of the problem.

What did the Beatles do in five years? They did the Beatles.

The Beatles carried that weight; they did the heavy lifting. They did what it took to get the results they wanted. Because that's what Decision #5 means: Achieving "top of the charts" success means putting in the work—sometimes hard work. But there's good news.

THE GOOD NEWS

Yes, Decision #5 means hard work. But the good news is this: If you take care of Decisions 1 through 4, Decision #5 will, in many cases, almost take care of itself. If you:

- *Spread the Spotlight* and make the *team* the star by bringing in diverse talents and sharing the credit;
- Create a *Single, Shared Vision*, get buy-in from your team, and show them how what they do fits into and supports the vision;
- *Play to Your Strengths*, and make sure each team member gets to do what they do best every day; and

- *Shake It Up* by challenging the rules, trying new things, and keeping it fun;

...in other words, if you and your team take the first four Decisions and make them your own, then *Carrying That Weight* to achieve your success will no longer seem an onerous chore. If a great team is allowed to do what they do best in the pursuit of a shared vision, and can have some fun along the way, they will naturally *want* to do what it takes to get there. Decision #5 becomes a natural offshoot of Decisions 1 through 4.

Paul McCartney once recalled writing the hit song *She Loves You* with John Lennon. "John and I wrote that one in a hotel room on an afternoon off. God bless [our] little cotton socks, [we] worked! Here I am talking about an afternoon off and we're sitting there writing! We just *loved it so much, it wasn't work!*"

Sometimes, when you take care of Decisions 1 through 4, Decision #5 takes care of itself.

A LESSON FROM SEINFELD

Before I became a keynote speaker, when I was a television producer, I had the good fortune to work with Jerry Seinfeld several times. On one of these occasions, we were sitting together in the green room (which, like virtually all green rooms everywhere, was painted a drab beige). He told me a story about a moment that changed his career.

One day, while he was a struggling young comedian in New York, Jerry decided he didn't feel like spending the day writing jokes. It was a nice day, so he chose to take a walk instead. While on his walk, he happened to see a construction crew that was just finishing its lunch break. As the workers returned to the job, Jerry thought to himself:

"Those guys don't want to go back to work. I'm sure they'd rather be taking a walk themselves. But instead, they're going back to work, because that's their job...that's what they do."

And with that, Jerry Seinfeld went back to his apartment and spent the day writing jokes…because that was his job. Instead of taking the day off, he made the decision to *carry the weight*…and he told me that *that*, more than anything else, is what made the difference in his career.

THE OTHER 20%

Woody Allen once said, "Eighty percent of success is showing up." Now, I'm a huge fan of Woody's…but with all due respect, "showing up" will only get you so far. Gerry and the Pacemakers "showed up." They're not the Beatles. A thousand other software companies "showed up." They're not Microsoft.

Yes, showing up will get you in the game. You may even stick around for a few innings. But the people who *win* the game—the ones who become legends—are the ones who target the other twenty percent.

I'll Carry That Weight...Right After My Nap

Good plan. No sense being a total idiot about this.

Oh don't look so relieved—I'm just kidding. Yes, carrying that weight can be hard. If it were easy, everybody would do it. But they don't, and that's good news. It's what gives you the advantage. It's your chance to go where they won't, to do what they're not willing to do. It's that margin, however slight, that makes all the difference.

Author and actress Carrie Fisher, who knows a thing or two about success, once noted, "There is no point at which you can say, 'Well, I'm successful now. I might as well take a nap.'" Success is a continuous process.

I'm not saying you can't pause every now and then to celebrate the victories along the way. In fact, I think you should do exactly this. It's part of making it fun. But if you find that these celebrations are being measured in months or years rather than hours or days, you may want to rethink your "celebratory nap" policy. A shark needs to keep moving forward or it will die. A business is no different (except that most businesses don't have such a prominent dorsal fin).

What are you going to do to move forward? Somebody once said, "The decisions made yesterday are responsible for the life of the company today. It's the decisions made today that will be responsible for the life of the company tomorrow." You could just as easily replace "the life of the company" with "your life." The point is, you must constantly be thinking of the next step. To use a baseball analogy, you can't steal second with your foot on first.

Most of us have a built-in resistance to carrying that weight. Whatever that weight is for us—starting a big project, finishing a big project, making a big decision—we resist it. We put it off. We're not willing to do what it takes. Steven Pressfield's best-selling book, *The War of Art*, is all about confronting this Resistance (the capitalization is Pressfield's) and defeating it. Yes, overcoming Resistance is hard. As Pressfield says, "Defeating Resistance is like giving birth. It seems absolutely impossible until you remember that women have been pulling it off successfully, with support and without, for fifty million years."

Overcoming resistance and carrying that weight are two sides of the same coin. Failure to do either is what keeps many of us from the "top of the charts."

The Beatles didn't rest after their first number one record. They got right to work on number two. Because the Beatles understood The Big Principle.

THE BIG PRINCIPLE

See, there's a principle that the universe operates on. It's a principle Jerry Seinfeld understood; it's a principle the Beatles understood. And the principle is this:

> *To a large degree, the results you get out of life will be equal to the effort you put in.*

Re-read the quote from Paul McCartney that started this chapter. "The reason we were twice as good as anyone else is because we worked twice as hard as anyone else." It's a perfect example of this principle in action.

People who don't "get" this principle don't read books like this. They're the ones who refuse to work harder because they're "not getting paid enough." They operate on the principle that things would get better if they could just "catch a break."

> *"The reason we were twice as good as anyone else is because we worked twice as hard as anyone else."*
> - Paul McCartney

You probably know people like this. Their attitude is, "I'd work harder if they'd pay me more money." These people are getting the equation backwards. They haven't figured it out yet. They don't realize that this is the equivalent of looking at a bare patch of earth and saying, "If you give me flowers, I'll give you water and fertilizer."

I have a friend in the speaking business who was complaining because she had to put together a marketing campaign for her services. She said she didn't want to do any marketing. I asked her what she *did* want. She said, "I just want people to hire me." She wanted the results without the effort. And she's not alone. A lot of people don't understand that the world doesn't operate that way.

They don't understand that their rewards will equal their effort, that they get out of life what they put into it, and that if they want to get more...they have to give more.

In short, they don't understand what the Beatles understood. In fact, the Beatles may have put it best...and I'm going to end with this (after one last "Top of the Charts" Challenge) because the Beatles ended with this...

"Top of the Charts" Challenge

1. What is one goal that you are currently working, either in your personal or professional life?

2. List the steps, in order, that it will take for you to reach this goal.

3. Are you willing to "carry that weight" and do the steps you just listed?

4. At work, what are some of the things you and your team are willing to do that the competition isn't? (And of course, we're talking about *legal, ethical* things only, right?)

5. Is there an area of your life that isn't where you would like it to be?

6. If so, what aren't you doing in that area that, if you did it, would make a positive difference? (A friend of mine once said, "Most of us know exactly what we need to do...*and just don't do it."*)

The 5 Best Decisions THE BEATLES Ever Made...

AND IN THE END...

And in the end...

"...the love you take is equal to the love you make."

\- The Beatles

The last album the four Beatles released together was *Let It Be*. But the last album the four Beatles actually *recorded* together was *Abbey Road. Abbey Road* was the last music the four Beatles ever made together. And, *as they originally designed it*[1], the last words of the last song of the last Beatles album were these:

---

[1] Although the last song on *Abbey Road* is actually *Her Majesty*, this was not the Beatles' original design. *Her Majesty* was originally going to be cut from the album, but a recording engineer stuck it onto the end of a test master (after a long silence so it wouldn't accidentally end up as part of the finished product!) just so it wouldn't get lost. Paul McCartney heard this test tape and liked it, so that's how the album was released.

And in the end...the love you take...
is equal to the love you make.

Folks, that's not a bad way to go out. That's not a bad way to cap off the most significant career in pop music history. But what does it mean...really?

Well, if you look at it in a broader sense, it means exactly what we've just been talking about. It means that, in the end, you get out of life what you put into it. Your results equal your efforts.

And in the end, the love you take is equal to the love you make.

It means: If you want to get more, you have to give more. And the giving comes first.

This is good news. In fact, it's great news. It means that we get to determine our outcomes. By changing the quality and quantity of our efforts, we change the quality and quantity of our results.

Does this mean that it's all going to be roses and cotton candy from now on? Nope. Bad stuff is going to happen. There are going to be setbacks. The Beatles had loads of them. They were turned down by virtually every recording company in London before finally getting a contract with a side label that specialized in, of all things, comedy records. There are going to be setbacks.

For the Beatles, the setbacks just meant that they had to try harder. They had to carry more weight. Because even then, they knew that their results would equal their efforts.

And in the end, the love you take is equal to the love you make.

We can't control the bad stuff. What we *can* control is how we deal with it. As my friend W Mitchell says, "It's not what happens to you...it's what you do about it." If we manage the front part of the equation, the back part will take care of itself. That's the way the Big Principle works.

So no more whining, no more griping, no more complaining. No more excuses. They won't work. What *will* work? The 5 Decisions we've talked about in this book:

1. *Spread the Spotlight:* Put together the strongest team you can, and be willing to share the credit.

2. *A Single, Shared Vision:* Define what it is that will emotionally (yet measurably) drive you and your team to your ultimate destination.

3. *Play to Your Strengths:* Discover, and focus on, the individual strengths of each of your team members. Decide what it is you do best…as an individual, as a team, and as an organization.

4. *Shake It Up!:* Ask questions like, "Is there a different way to do what I'm doing?" "Is there a *better* way?" (And don't forget to have fun!)

5. *Carry That Weight:* Decide where you want to go. Obtain the tools you'll need to get there. Put in the

time. In virtually all cases, your rewards will equal your effort.

You get out of life what you put into it.

So, if you want to get more:

- in your career
- in your community
- in your relationships

...you have to give more.

Because, in the end, the love you take *is* equal to the love you make.

Bill's Top 10 Beatles Books

1. Philip Norman, **Shout!: The Beatles in Their Generation,** Fireside Books
2. The Beatles, **The Beatles Anthology,** Chronicle Books
3. Mark Lewisohn, **The Complete Beatles Chronicle,** Hamlyn Books
4. Mark Lewisohn, **The Complete Beatles Recording Sessions,** Three Rivers Press
5. Hunter Davies, **The Beatles,** W. W. Norton & Company
6. Tim Riley, **Tell Me Why: The Beatles: Album by Album,** Da Capo Press
7. Andy Babiuk, **Beatles Gear,** Backbeat Books
8. Larry Kane, **Ticket to Ride,** Running Press Book Publishers
9. Nicholas Schaffner, **Beatles Forever,** McGraw-Hill
10. Mark Hertsgaard, **A Day in the Life: The Music and Artistry of the Beatles,** Delta

10 Things You Probably Didn't Know About the Beatles

1. John Lennon and Paul McCartney once booked themselves as a duo called The Nerk Twins.
2. The harmonica John plays on *Love Me Do* was shoplifted from a store in Holland.
3. The refrain of "very strange" in the song *Penny Lane* is an inside joke; there was a father-son law office there called "Strange & Strange."
4. The Beatles once lost a talent competition to a woman who played the spoons.
5. One female fan trying to get backstage at a Seattle Beatles concert fell 25 feet down a ventilation duct and landed at Ringo's feet.
6. The Beatles were the first rock and roll band to play Carnegie Hall, but Carnegie Hall thought they were getting a classical group, as the Beatles had been booked as "a British quartet."
7. The Beatles and the Rolling Stones had a tacit agreement not to release their recordings at the same time.

8. Erich Segal, the author of *Love Story*, was one of the writers for the Beatles' film, *Yellow Submarine*.
9. The original title for the *Rubber Soul* album was *The Magic Circle*.
10. John's song, *Good Morning, Good Morning*, was inspired by a corn flake commercial.

About the Author

Bill Stainton

Bill is a multiple Emmy Award winning TV producer, performer, and writer; a popular keynote speaker; and an internationally-recognized Beatles expert.

Not bad for a kid who grew up behind a dairy farm in the Amish countryside of Lancaster, Pennsylvania.

The owner of two businesses, and a 20+-year veteran of corporate management, Bill is also the author of nine corporate training programs which are distributed worldwide.

As a keynote speaker (and former president of the Northwest chapter of the National Speakers Association), Bill has entertained and enlightened thousands with his Customized Humorous Keynotes, as well as his popular programs on humor, creativity...and, of course, *The 5 Best Decisions the Beatles Ever Made!*

Ovation Consulting Group, Inc.
4522 131st Place SW
Mukilteo, WA 98275
425-741-3972 • 888-5BEATLE
Fax: 425-742-2881
www.OvationConsulting.com
email: Bill@OvationConsulting.com